JAZZ TRACKS

The **ultimate backing track** collection for guitar

ROBERT BROWN
MARK DZIUBA
JODY FISHER

Alfred, the leader in educational music publishing, and the National Guitar Workshop, one of America's finest guitar schools, have joined forces to bring you the best, most progressive educational tools possible. We hope you will enjoy this book and encourage you to look for other fine products from Alfred and the National Guitar Workshop.

This book was acquired, edited, and produced by Workshop Arts, Inc., the publishing arm of the National Guitar Workshop.
Nathaniel Gunod, acquisitions, managing editor
Burgess Speed, senior editor
Timothy Phelps, interior design
Ante Gelo, music typesetter
CD recorded at Standing Room Only Recording Studio, Fontana, CA; and Workshop Sounds Studio, Cranford, NJ
Engineered by Darrell Ashley, Robert Brown, and Mark Dziuba
Music composed by Robert Brown, Mark Dziuba, and Jody Fisher
Guitars: Robert Brown, Mark Dziuba, and Jody Fisher
Keyboards: Scott Smith, Robert Brown, and Mark Dziuba
Bass: Jeff Stover, Robert Brown, and Mark Dziuba
Drums: Ron Dunn-Jones
Saxophone: Glen Myerscough

Cover photographs: Lead Guitar: © Gibson / Courtesy of Gibson USA • Bass Guitar: © Schecter / Courtesy of Schecter • Drums: © Drum Workshop / Courtesy of Drum Workshop • Keyboard: © Yamaha / Courtesy of Yamaha Music • Background © dreamstime.com / Beholdereye

Alfred Music Publishing Co., Inc.
P.O. Box 10003
Van Nuys, CA 91410-0003
alfred.com

ISBN-10: 0-7390-8604-9 (Book & CD)
ISBN-13: 978-0-7390-8604-9 (Book & CD)

Contents

Introduction

Many consider practicing a necessary evil, a chore, or BORING! Endless scales and arpeggios are important but, unfortunately, they sometimes get tedious. Perhaps the most enjoyable way to practice techniques is by incorporating them into your solos while you jam. *Jazz Tracks* is the ideal tool to provide accompaniments and techniques that will improve your playing while you solo.

There are over 30 tunes included that range from simple to complex, all in the styles of the seminal artists from the history of jazz, including classic progressions in the style of songs by artists and songwriters like Larry Carlton, Miles Davis, Roberta Flack, Freddie Hubbard, Chaka Khan, Johnny Mercer, Charles Mingus, and many more. There are also simple modal progressions for you to jam over. You won't just be practicing techniques, you will actually be crafting your own authentic jazz sound.

This book provides lead sheets that include tips and scales, and original MP3 accompaniment tracks let you stretch out and experiment as your chops develop. Scales and modes are recommended for every tune, shown using standard music notation, TAB, or guitar neck diagrams. Rhythmic notation and riffs are provided for select tunes.

Jazz Tracks is the perfect way for you to make the most out of your practice time and seriously advance your improvisational skills. Stop being bored and start to enjoy practicing right now!

About the Authors

Robert Brown, a guitarist and composer, was on the faculty of the National Guitar Summer Workshop from 1984 to 1991. During those years, he taught everything from blues to jazz, songwriting, and MIDI seminars. He is the author of many other books published by the National Guitar Workshop and Alfred Music Publishing. Robert Brown is currently living and working in Nashville, TN.

Mark Dziuba, a guitarist, bassist, and composer, received his master of music degree in theory and composition from the University of Illinois in 1987. While there, he attended workshops and lectures with composers such as John Cage, Milton Babbitt, and Vladimir Ussachevsky. He currently serves on the music faculty of the State University of New York at New Paltz. Mark is a senior faculty member of the National Guitar Summer Workshop where he has worked with John Scolfield, Ronnie Earl, Tal Farlow, Mark Egan, and Larry Carlton.

Jody Fisher has worked professinally in virtually all styles of music during his career, from straight ahead and contemporary jazz to rock 'n' roll, country, and pop. He has taught guitar and jazz studies at the University of Redlands and the Idyllwild School of Music and the Arts (ISOMATA). An active performer in the Southern California area, he maintains a private teaching practice and is a director of the National Guitar Workshop.

How to Use This Book and MP3 CD

This book and CD allows you to be the lead guitarist in a band. You'll play solos with a great rhythm section backing you up.

For each tune on the CD, you will be given the following information:

1. The key

2. How many choruses there are

3. When other soloists will play

4. The chord progression

In the book, each chord progression is followed by scale diagrams. Use them as a guide to help you improvise.

1. The tonic of each scale is displayed as a white dot.

2. Most scales and modes are shown using one position.

3. When scales are displayed using the whole fretboard, at first, break the scale into four or five fret sections, this will make it much easier to manage the scale.

Here are some suggestions that will make your practice time more effective:

- Spend some time just listening to each track.

- Pay attention to the form each piece takes (repeats, coda, etc.).

- Learn the notes as well as the shape of each scale on the fingerboard.

- Sing your solos before you play them (great for ear training).

Tuning

 Track 1 Make sure your guitar is in tune with this MP3 CD by tuning to this track.

Tune Me

This tune is a medium tempo swing groove based on Miles Davis's "Tune Up" that changes key every four measures. It begins in the key of D, then moves to C, B♭, and back to D. Two modes to try are Dorian and Mixolydian: both shown below in the key of D. When the key changes to C, play D Dorian and G Mixolydian. In other words, play a whole step (two frets) down from E Dorian and A Mixolydian. Then, move another whole step down for the key of B♭. Listen to the 2nd guitar solo and you'll get the idea.

E Dorian

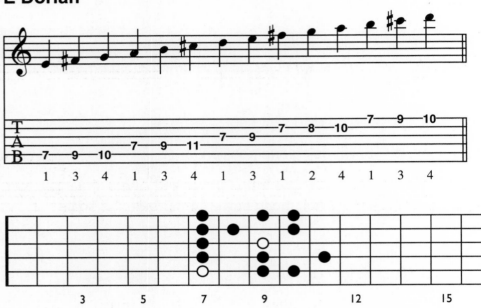

A Mixolydian

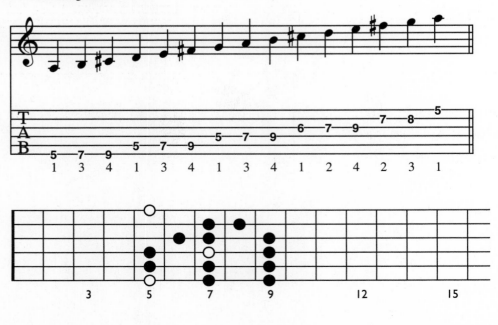

Play 13 times

Em7 ⋯ A7 ⋯ Dmaj7 ⋯ %

5 Dm7 ⋯ G7 ⋯ Cmaj7 ⋯ %

9 Cm7 ⋯ F7 ⋯ B♭maj7 ⋯ %

Last time to Coda

13 Em7 ⋯ A7 ⋯ Dmaj7 ⋯ Em7 ⋯ A7

17 Em7 ⋯ A7 ⋯ Dmaj7 ⋯ Em7 ⋯ A7

21 Em7 ⋯ A7 ⋯ Dmaj7 ♯11

Form

Verse 1: One *chorus* (a chorus is one time through the form) of the 2nd guitar solo—you *comp* (play the chord changes).

Verse 2: One chorus of guitar solo—2nd guitar comps.

Verse 3: Three choruses of guitar solo.

Verse 4: Two choruses of piano solo—you comp.

Verse 5: Four choruses of guitar solo.

Verse 6: One chorus of bass solo—you comp.

Verse 7: One chorus of guitar solo.

Verse 8: End.

Track 3

A New Blue

This is a 16-measure bossa nova in the style of Kenny Dorham's "Blue Bossa" which moves through several different keys. The first eight measures are in the key of C minor, the next four measures are in D♭ major, and the last four are in C minor. You could play the whole tune in eighth position by using C Aeolian for C Minor and C Locrian for D♭ Major. Be sure to *listen* to what you are playing! Here's something to ask yourself: when can I use A or A♭? B or B♭?

C Aeolian

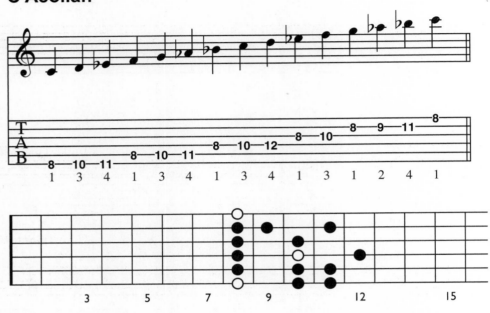

C Locrian

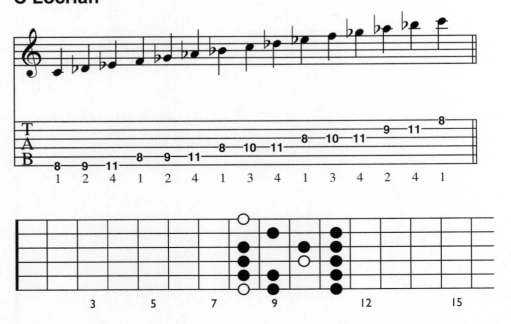

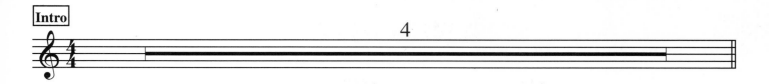

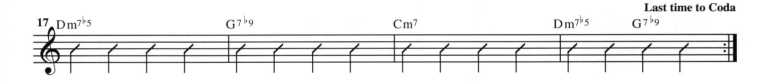

Form

Verse 1: Intro—four measures.

Verse 2: One chorus of 2nd guitar solo—you comp.

Verse 3: Four choruses of guitar solo.

Verse 4: Two choruses of electric piano solo—you comp.

Verse 5: Five choruses of guitar solo.

Verse 6: End—Cmin vamp.

In the Fall

This is a medium tempo swing tune in the style of Johnny Mercer's "Autumn Leaves." The form is AAB, which means the A section (the first eight measures) is played twice before moving on to the B section. Try using G Major, F♯ Locrian, D Mixolydian, and E Aeolian as the scales to improvise with. When you get to the last four chords of the B section, start by playing the 3rd and 7th of each chord. These would be:

    G and D over the Emin7
    G and D♭ over the E♭7
    F and C over the Dmin7
    F and C♭ (B) over the D♭7

Try to create a nice musical line or melody using those notes. Another example would be to use the 5th and the 9th of each chord:

    B and F♯ over the Emin7
    B♭ and F over the E♭7
    A and E over the Dmin7
    A♭ and E♭ over the D♭7

G Major

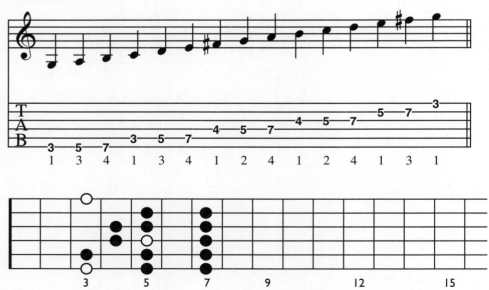

F♯ Locrian

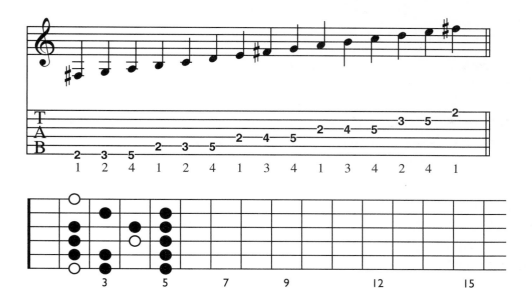

D Mixolydian

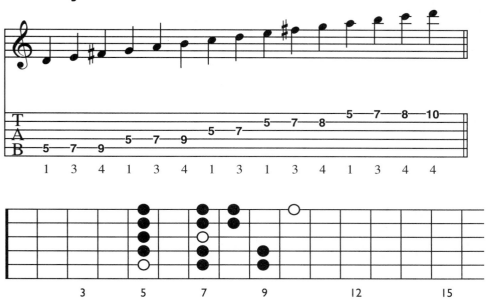

E Aeolian

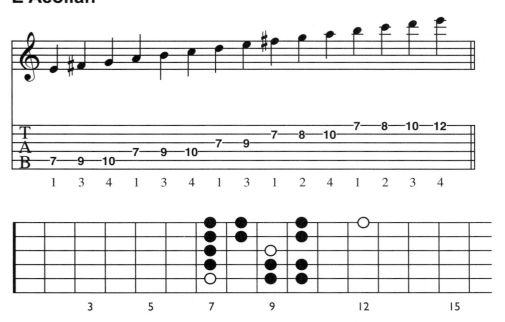

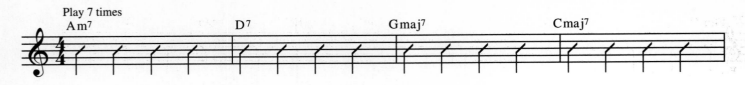

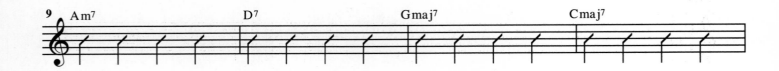

Form

Verse 1: Three choruses of guitar solo.

Verse 2: One chorus of piano solo—you comp.

Verse 3: Three choruses of guitar solo.

Verse 4: End.

Feets

This tune is a jazz waltz, which means it is in $\frac{3}{4}$ time instead of $\frac{4}{4}$ time. It is in a style very similar to Wayne Shorter's "Footprints." The trickiest part of the tune is the F#7 to F7. Use the 3rd and 7th of each chord as a point of departure for your soloing: for F#7, use A# and E; for F7, use A and E♭. You can also try using an E Aeolian scale for the whole tune except for the F# to F7 progression, where you can use F# and F Mixolydian scales.

E Aeolian

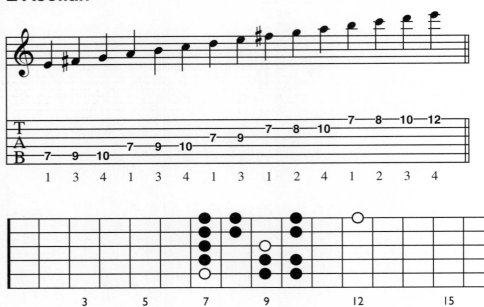

F# Mixolydian

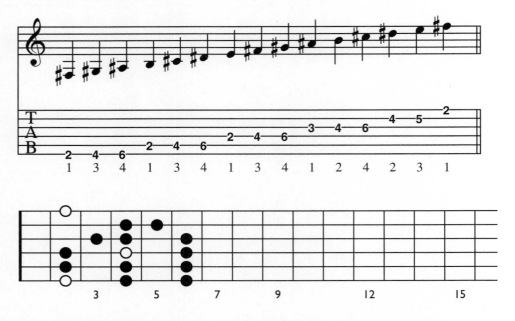

Note: For F Mixolydian, simply move the F# Mixolydian fingering down a half step.

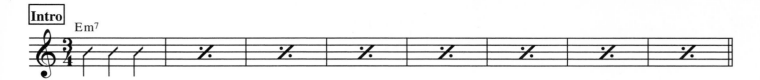

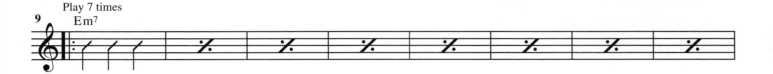

Form

    Verse 1: Intro—eight measures.

    Verse 2: Three choruses of guitar solo.

    Verse 3: One chorus of piano solo—you comp.

    Verse 4: Three choruses of guitar solo.

    Verse 5: End.

Birdy

A medium tempo swing tune in the style of Tad Dameron's "Lady Bird," this song will take you through the keys of C, E♭, A♭, and G. Concentrate and watch out for the iimin7/V7 chords like Amin7/D7 to figure out where the key changes are. Use the ♭5 note on B♭7♭5 (F♭) and E♭7♭5 (B♭♭) because they are the notes that really give the chords their particular sound or color. Try using a C Major scale for those measures in the key of C and an A♭ Major scale for those measures in the key of A♭.

C Major

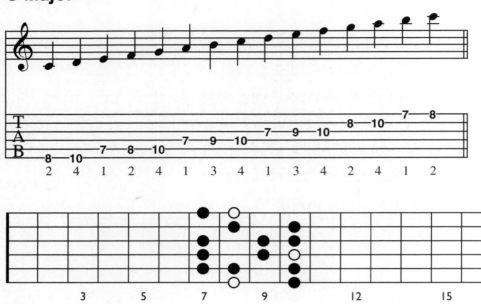

A♭ Major

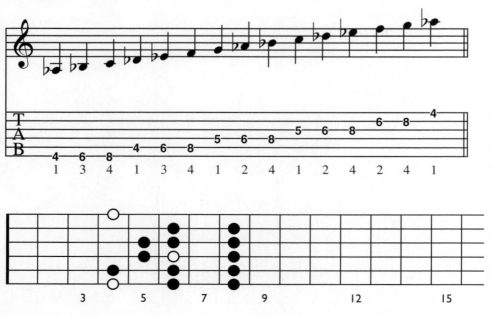

Form

Verse 1: Five choruses of guitar solo.

Verse 2: One chorus of piano solo—you comp.

Verse 3: Two choruses of piano solo.

Verse 4: One chorus of trading two's (soloists alternately improvising every two measures).

Verse 5: One chorus of bass solo—you comp.

Verse 6: One chorus of guitar solo.

Verse 7: End.

Night Walker

This tune is basically a minor blues in the style of Joe Henderson's "Out of the Night" but with more sophisticated chord changes. You will have to listen and analyze in order to play the correct notes. For example, at the end of measure 4 you will have to play a G♯ for the E7 chord. In measure nine, the C9 has a B♭ in it, and in measure 11, the F7 has an E♭. You can also start by using E Aeolian and E Blues Pentatonic scales. Writing out the 3rd and the 7th for each chord will help you know the important notes to target in your solo.

E Aeolian

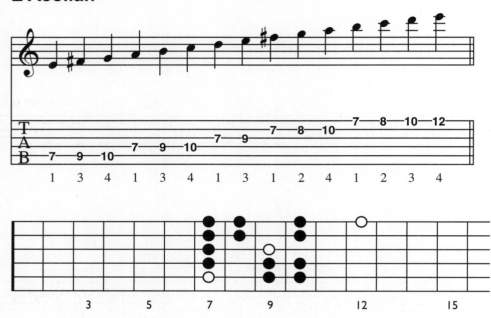

E Blues Pentatonic

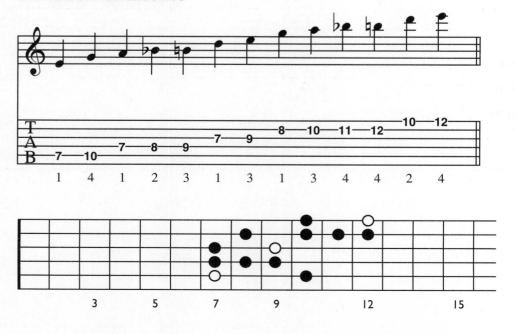

Form

Verse 1: Five choruses of guitar solo.

Verse 2: Two choruses of organ solo—you comp.

Verse 3: Five choruses of guitar solo.

Verse 4: End.

Greenish Blue

This is a ballad in the style of Miles Davis's "Blue in Green." It is tricky because the form is 10 measures long, so you have to pay attention to where you are all the time. The tune is basically in the key of D Minor, but there are a lot of B♭'s so you could also think in F Major. Try soloing with B♭ Lydian and D Aeolian scales.

B♭ Lydian

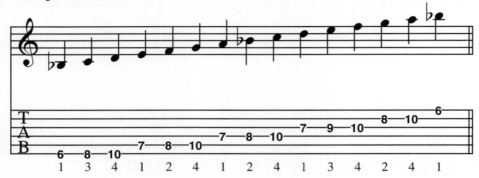

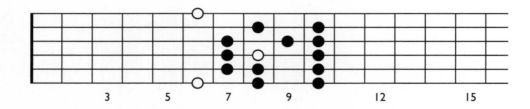

D Aeolian

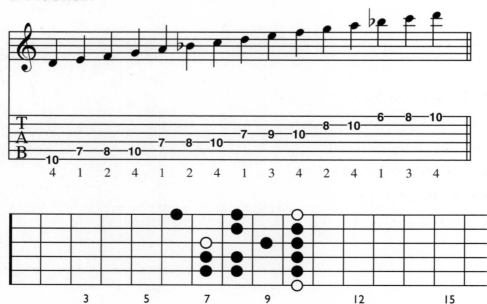

Form

Verse 1: One chorus of 2nd guitar solo—you comp.

Verse 2: Two choruses of guitar solo.

Verse 3: Three choruses of guitar solo—double time.

Verse 4: Two choruses of vibes solo—you comp.

Verse 5: One chorus of bass solo—you comp.

Verse 6: One chorus of guitar solo—half time.

Verse 7: End.

Tape Me

Here's another bossa nova for you in the style of Joe Henderson's "Recordame." It is also pretty tricky, so listen to the audio and analyze the harmony. Where are the different key centers? We start the tune in A Minor, go to C Minor, then to B♭, A♭, G♭, and F before going back to A Minor. Whew! Try using a B Locrian scale over A Minor and C Dorian over the measures using C Minor through B♭maj7.

B Locrian

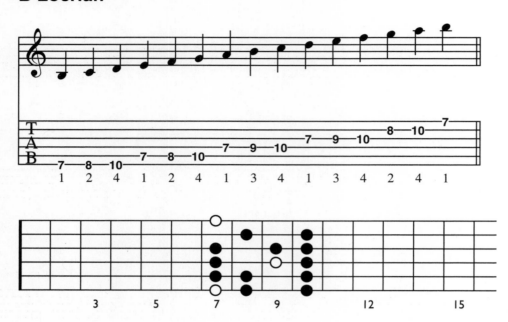

C Dorian

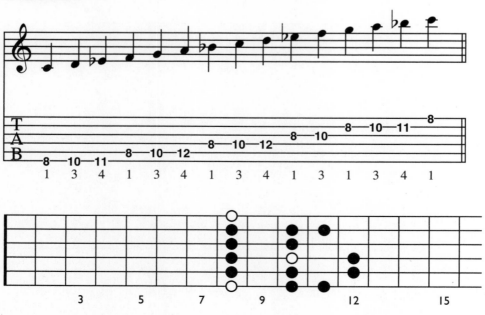

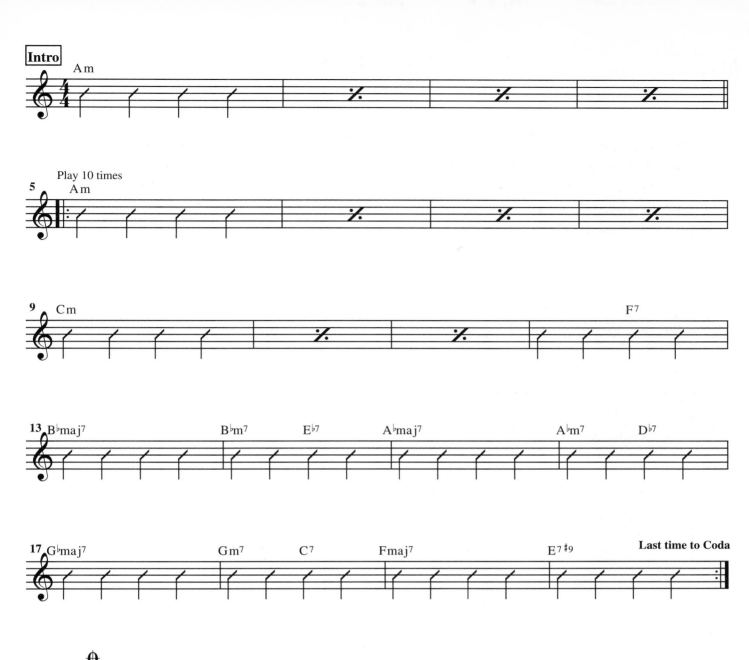

Form

Verse 1: Intro–four measures.

Verse 2: Four choruses of guitar solo.

Verse 3: One chorus of guitar solo–double time.

Verse 4: One chorus of piano solo–you comp.

Verse 5: Four choruses of guitar solo–half time.

Verse 6: End.

Things Change

This is a blues based on Charles Mingus's "Things Ain't What They Used to Be." The chord changes are on pages 26 and 27. The chords on page 26 are used for the melody or solos at the beginning and end of the tune. The chords on page 27 are to be used while soloing. It will be easier if you remember that this is a 12-measure blues. G Mixolydian, G Blues Pentatonic, and E Blues Pentatonic scales will all work well. Also, don't miss that diminished seventh chord!

G Mixolydian

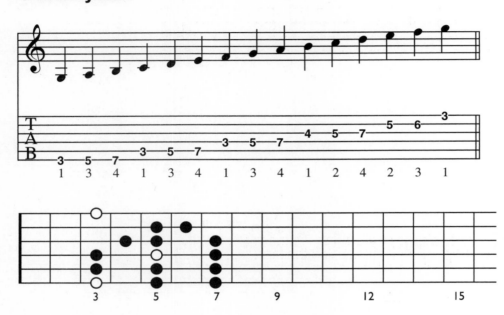

G Blues Pentatonic

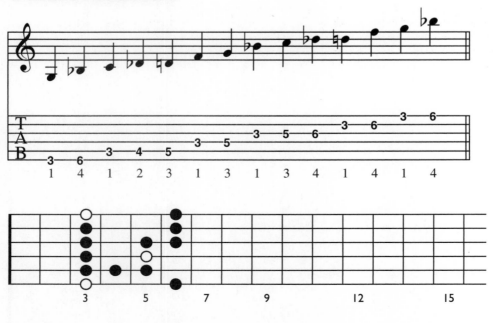

E Blues Pentatonic

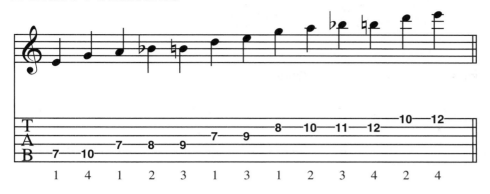

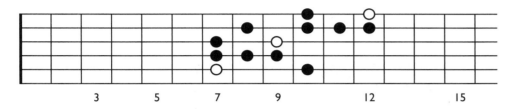

C# Diminished

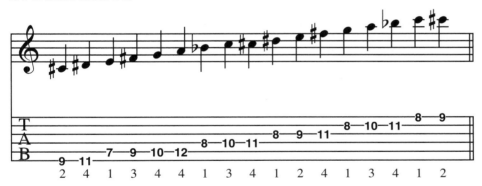

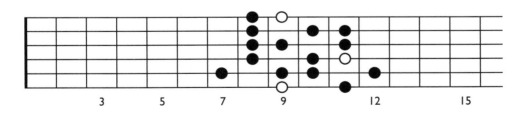

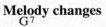

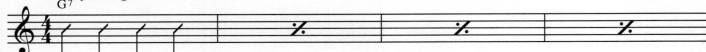

Form

Verse 1: Five choruses of guitar solo.

Verse 2: Two choruses of organ solo—you comp.

Verse 3: Five choruses of guitar solo.

Verse 4: End.

Solo changes
Play 12 times

After solos, D.C. al Coda

Shake Me

This is a long, 54-measure Latin tune based on "Shaker Song." The tune starts off in the key of C, moves to E♭, to D♭, back to E♭, and C. All of this happens in the A section. Can you see where those key changes are? Find them! Notice that the B section jumps between F and C, so you need to decide where to play B and where to play B♭. The changes go by pretty fast, so make sure you get the ⅱmin7/V7 each time it happens.

C Major

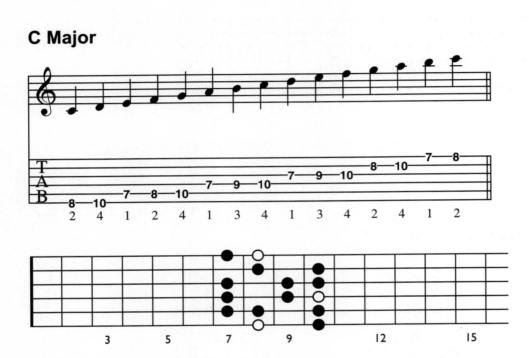

C Aeolian

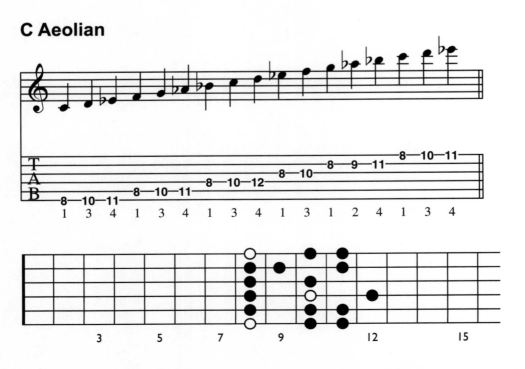

C Locrian

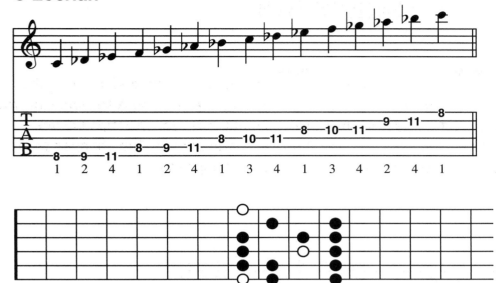

Here are a few chords you may not know:

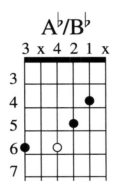
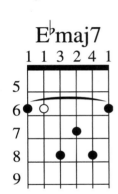
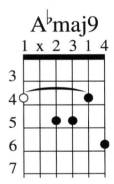

Form

Verse 1: Two choruses of guitar solo.

Verse 2: One chorus of electric piano solo—you comp.

Verse 3: One chorus of guitar solo.

Verse 4: End.

Feel Like Makin' Lunch

This tune is typical of the way some contemporary jazz artists enjoy using pop songs as part of their repertoire. Songs by Roberta Flack and many older Motown pieces are currently being recorded by the smooth jazz community. Improvise using an E♭ Major Pentatonic scale over the entire progression except when the D♭9♯11 chord appears. Then try using the D♭ Whole Tone scale.

E♭ Major Pentatonic

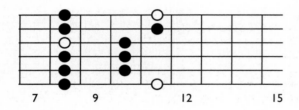

D♭ Whole Tone

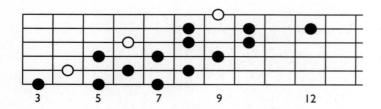

Form
Play the entire form five times. Play rhythm on the 3rd chorus while the guitar solos.

Help Me Remember

This is a "groove" tune. Many smooth jazz songs lock into a steady groove with kicks and accents placed in strategic places. Listen to artists like Grover Washington, Jr. for examples of this style. Improvise using the D Super Locrian scale for the D7#5#9, Db Whole Tone for Db9#11, Db Major for the Dbmaj9, C Major for the Cmaj9, and G Whole Tone for G7#5. G Minor Pentatonic will work well over everything else.

G Minor Pentatonic

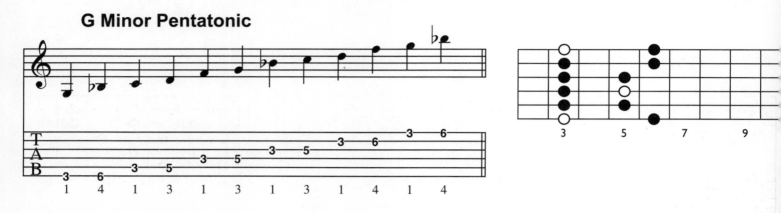

D Super Locrian

Db Whole Tone

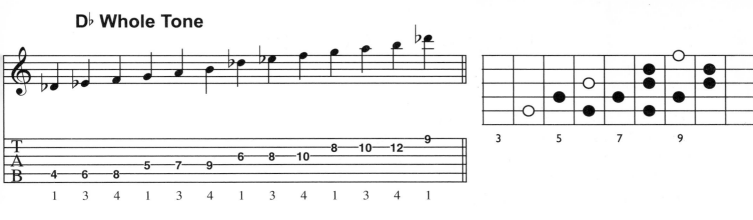

G Whole Tone

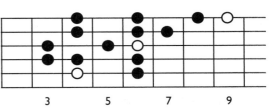

Db Major

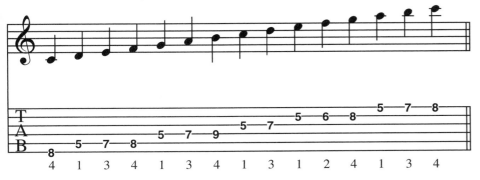
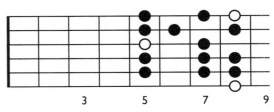

C Major

Form

Play the entire form three times. Play rhythm on the 2nd chorus while the sax solos.

 Track 14

Ballad Measure

"Ballad Measure" is typical of the kind of jazz/pop ballad you might hear on a smooth jazz album when a vocal track is included. Listen to Chaka Khan and Nathan East with Fourplay, or even Toni Braxton, for tasteful examples of this style. Use a C Major scale for the A section. In the B section, use E♭ Major for the first two measures, then D♭ Major for the first ending and go back to C Major for the second ending. In the C section, use an F Major scale for measures 1, 3, 4, 5, and 8. E Super Locrian works well over the E7♯9 in measure 2. C Major works in measures 6 and 7. Use A Minor Pentatonic for the second ending.

C Major

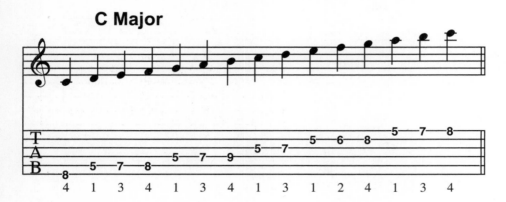
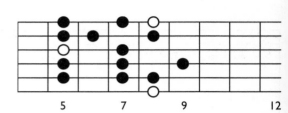

F Major

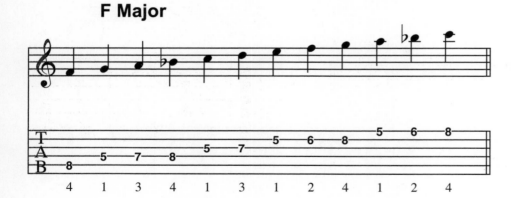
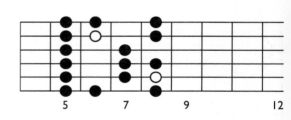

E♭ Major

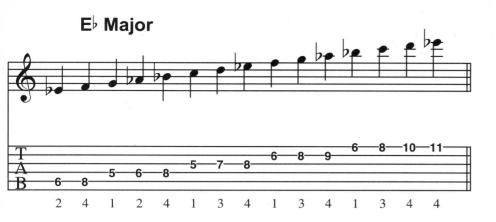
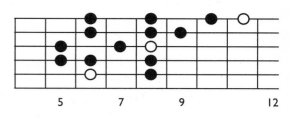

D♭ Major

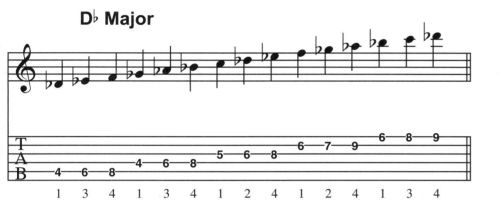
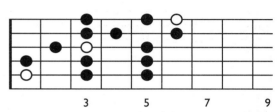

A Minor Pentatonic

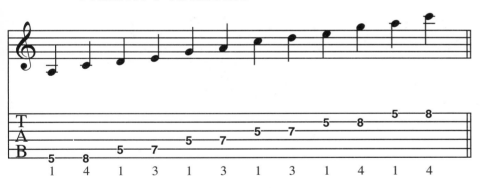
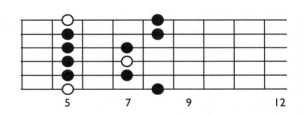

E Super Locrian

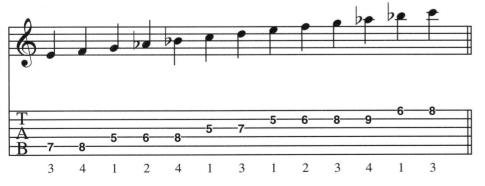
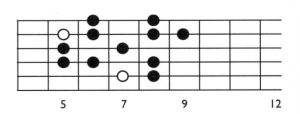

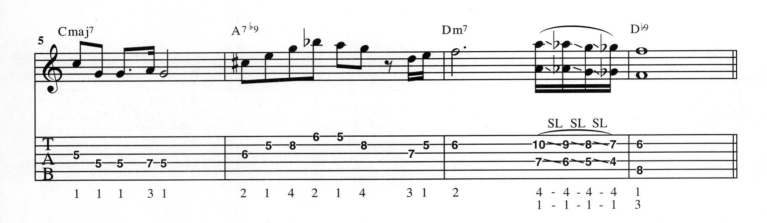

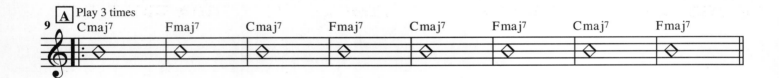

Form

Play the entire form three times. Play rhythm on the A and B sections in the 2nd chorus while the guitar solos.

Early Afternoon

Latin rhythms, along with rhythms from other cultural and ethnic styles, have heavily influenced contemporary jazz. For inspiration, listen to Clare Fischer's "Morning" or just about any recording from Spyro Gyra. In the A section of this tune, use a B♭ Minor Pentatonic scale for the first two measures and repeat. In the B section, go back to B♭ Minor Pentatonic for four measures and repeat. In the second ending, play B Mixolydian over the B7 and slide it down one fret to match the B♭7.

B♭ Minor Pentatonic

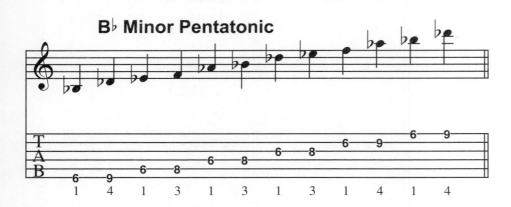
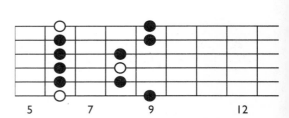

D♭ Major

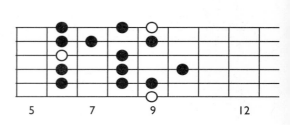

B Mixolydian

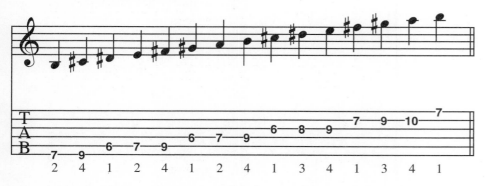
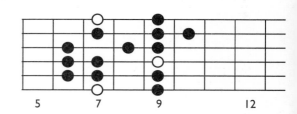

Form

Play along with the Intro. Play the rest of the form five times. Play rhythm on the 3rd chorus while the keyboard solos.

Last Dawn

"Last Dawn" is in the style of songs composed by Herbie Hancock and Freddie Hubbard. In the A section, use an A♭ Minor Pentatonic scale (transpose the B♭ Minor Pentatonic on page 42) or possibly a G♭ Major scale but change the root of the A♭ Major scale (see page 16) to G♭ by lowering everything two frets. The B section contains mostly maj7♯11 chords over which a Lydian scale starting at the root of the chord is the best choice. B Whole Tone scale (see page 35, but change the root of the G Whole Tone scale to B) fits the B7♭5, while B Mixolydian (page 42) works well over the B7. Use E♭ Super Locrian over the E♭7♭9.

E Lydian

G Lydian

C Lydian

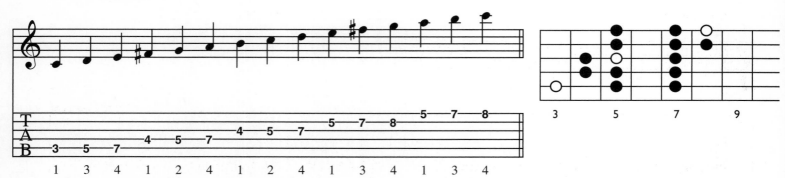

Form

Play along with the Intro . Play the rest of the form six times. Play rhythm on the 3rd chorus while the keyboard solos.

Track 17

Louie the Lizard

Larry Carlton is considered by many to be one of the most tasteful players of the smooth jazz style. "Louie the Lizard" is based on the type of chord progression you might find Larry soloing over. Use the D Major Pentatonic scale over the A section. The F Major Pentatonic scale can be used over measures 1, 2, and 4 in the B section. For a change, you might try C Major Pentatonic over the FMaj7 in the first measure of the B section. You can also try E♭ or B♭ Major Pentatonic over the E♭maj7 in the third measure of the section. Return to D Major Pentatonic for the C section.

D Major Pentatonic

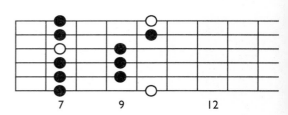

F Major Pentatonic

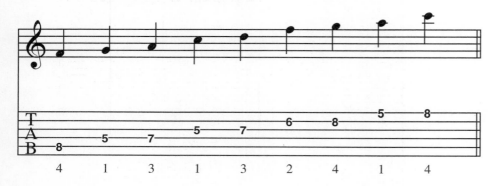
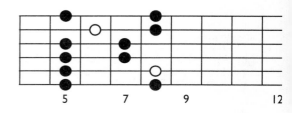

E♭ Major Pentatonic

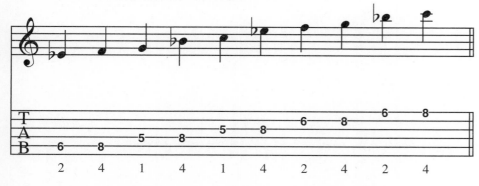
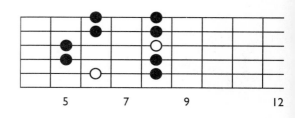

Form

Play along with the Intro . Play the rest of the form five times. Play rhythm on the 3rd chorus while the sax solos.

Esmeralda

The jazz samba has been a mainstay throughout the history of jazz. Jazz musicians like Airto, Flora Purim, and others have based much of their sound on this style. Use C Minor Pentatonic for the entire A section. An A♭ Major scale will work fine over the first two measures (including the repeat) of the B section. G Major will take care of measures 3 and 4 of the B section before returning to the C Minor Pentatonic scale in the last two measures.

C Minor Pentatonic

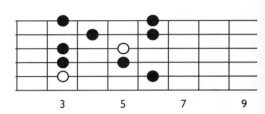

A♭ Major

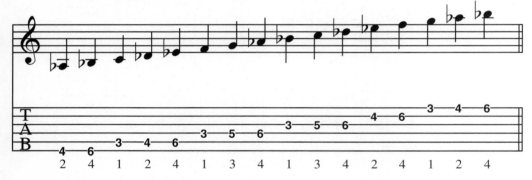
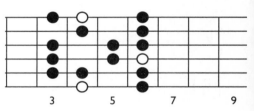

G Major

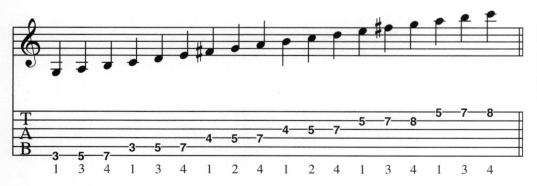
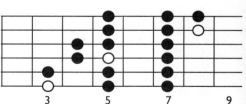

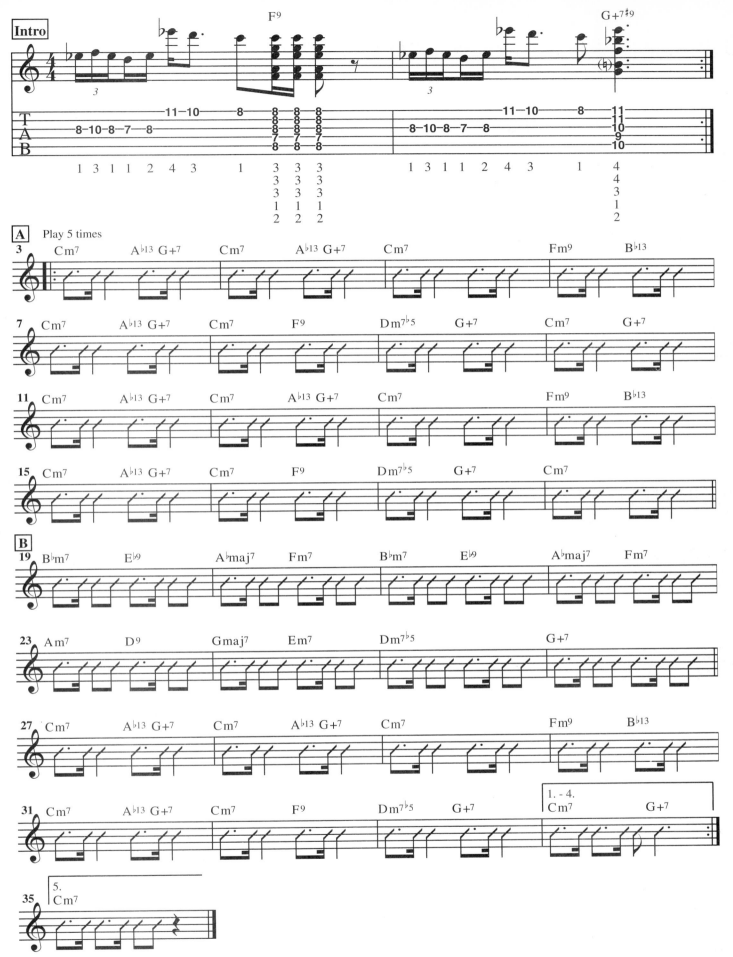

Form

Play along with the Intro . Play the rest of the form five times. Play rhythm on the 3rd chorus while the guitar solos.

Big Baby

"Big Baby" demonstrates a more modern, straight eighth-note feel. Use a G Mixolydian over each G7 chord, as well as the Dm11 that appears in measure 18. The F Major scale will work over every Fmaj7 chord, as well as all measures featuring Gm7 to C9. Use G Harmonic Minor in all measures featuring Am7♭5 to D7. B♭ Major goes with measures 12, 28, and 44, as well as the first halves of measures 13, 14, 29, 30, 45, and 46. Use a C♯ Diminished scale for each C♯dim chord and use a D♭ Major Pentatonic for the D♭maj7 chord.

G Mixolydian

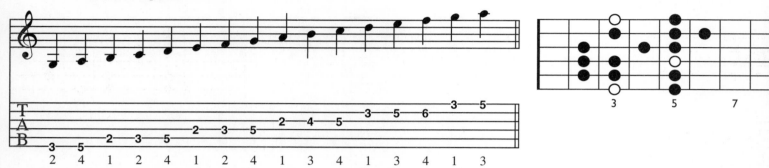

F Major

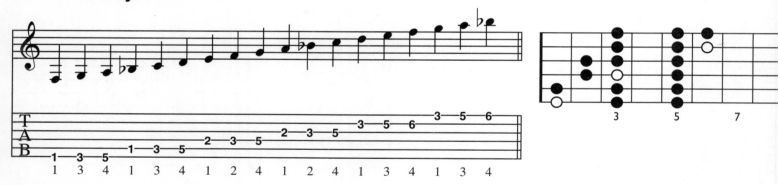

G Harmonic Minor

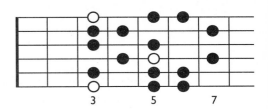

B♭ Major

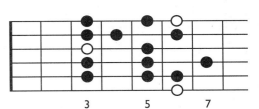

C♯ Diminished

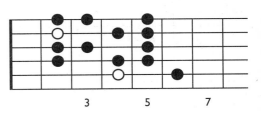

D♭ Major Pentatonic

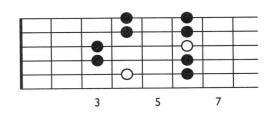

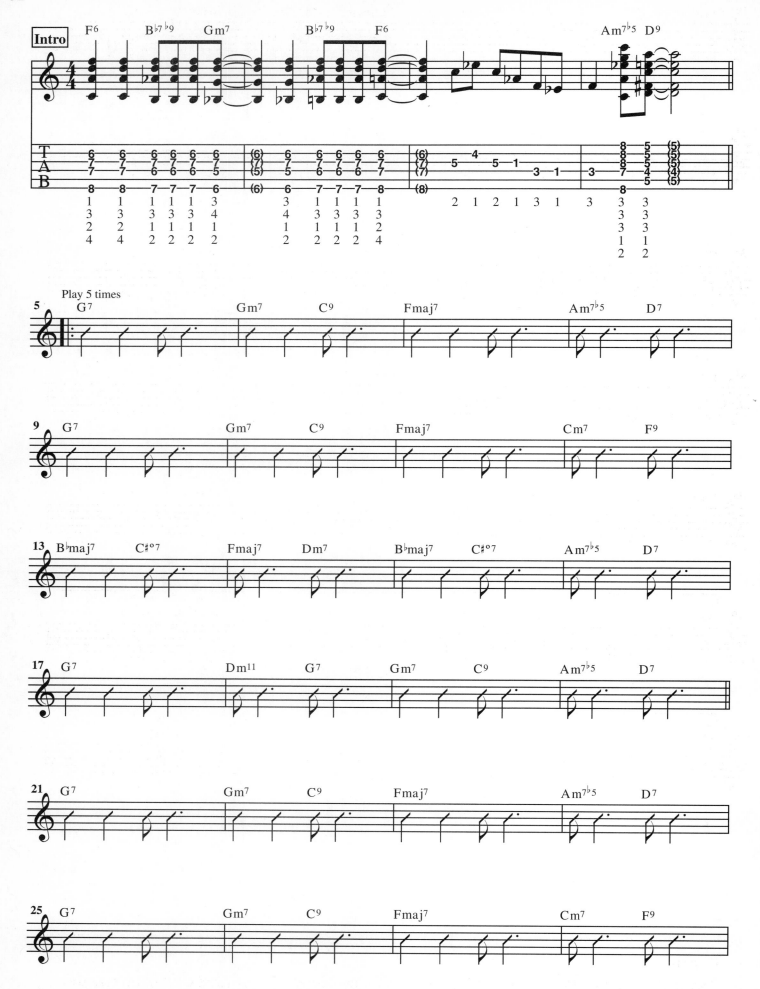

Form

Play along with the Intro . Play the rest of the form five times. Play rhythm on the 3rd chorus while the sax solos.

Mutual Infraction

Here's a basic ballad in a contemporary jazz context. For measures 3, 14, and the last two beats of 16, use a B♭ Major scale. Use an F Major scale for measure 5. Measures 6 and 7 work well with an E♭ Major scale. Use a D♭ Major scale for measures 8 and 9. Use a B Major scale for measures 10, 11, 15 and the first two beats of 16. Use a C Major scale for measure 13. Try a G Harmonic Minor scale for measure 4 and B♭ Harmonic minor for measure 12. For a slightly edgier sound, replace all major scales with major pentatonic scales. Here are the scales needed for this tune from the root B♭.

B♭ Major

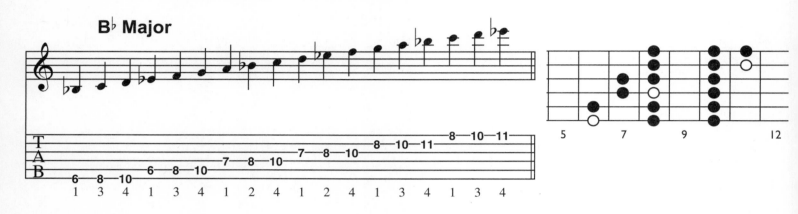

B♭ Major Pentatonic

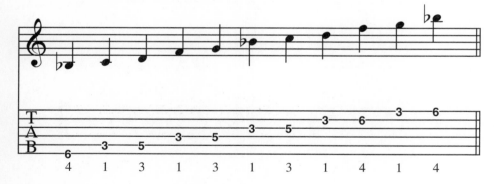

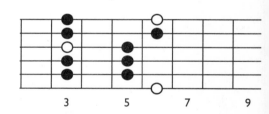

B♭ Harmonic Minor

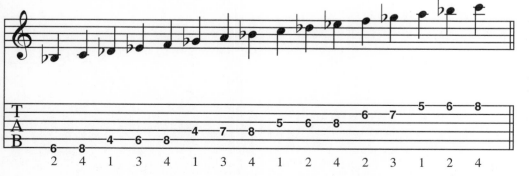

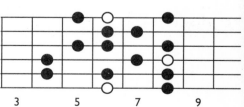

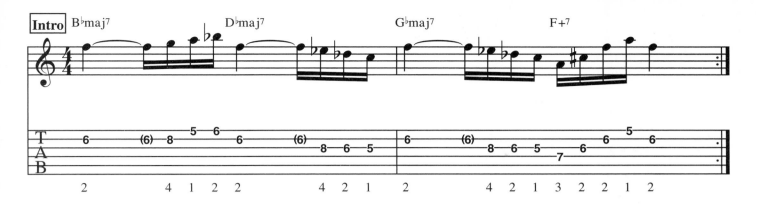

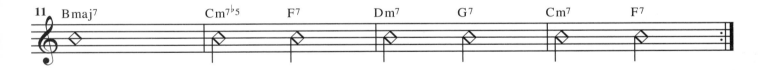

Form
Play along with the Intro . Play the rest of the form six times. Play rhythm on the 3rd chorus while the guitar solos, and on the 5th chorus, while the keyboard solos.

56

Wes Montgomery *(1923–1968) was one of the most important jazz guitarists, emerging after such seminal figures as Django Reinhardt and Charlie Christian. He influenced countless others, including Pat Martino, George Benson, Emily Remler, Kenny Burrell, and Pat Metheny.*

***Joe Pass** (1929–1994) was known for his extensive use of walking bass lines, melodic counterpoint during improvisation, use of a chord/melody style of playing, and outstanding knowledge of chord progressions. He opened up new possibilities for jazz guitar and had a profound influence on future guitarists.*

All Three of Us

One characterstic unique to smooth jazz is the use of a repeating chord progression to establish a groove throughout a tune. Check out David Sanborn and Kenny G for good examples of this.

There are several ways to improvise over "All Three of Us." One way would be to play A Minor Pentatonic over the A and C sections, and C Mixolydian over the B and D sections. Another way would be to use an F Major scale for A and C and then switch to E Super Locrian for the E7#9.

F Major

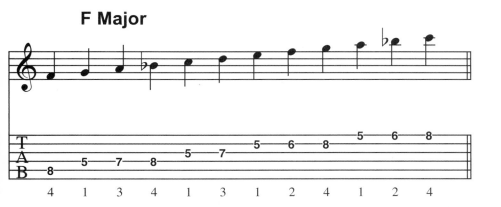
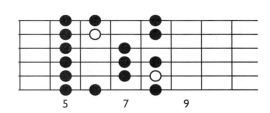

C Mixolydian

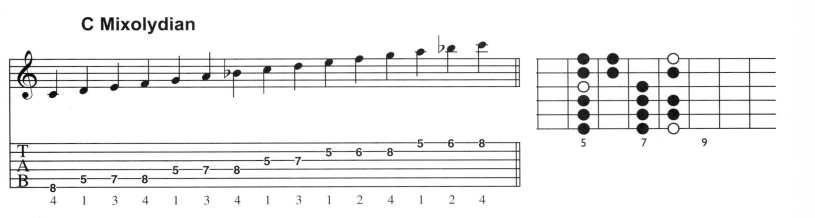

E Super Locrian

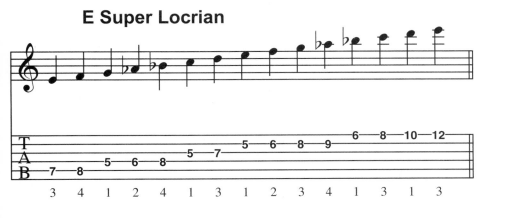
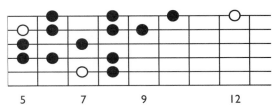

Form

Play along with the Intro . Play the rest of the form five times. Play rhythm on the 3rd chorus while the sax solos.

The tracks from pages 60–85 are intended to help you work on one scale or progression at a time. Get creative and really stretch out with these tracks.

Track 22

Dorian to Mixolydian

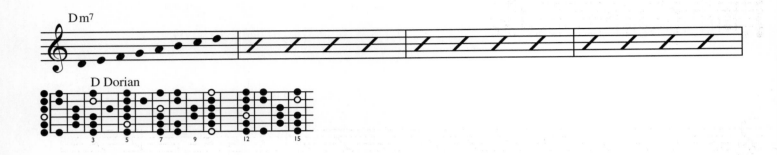

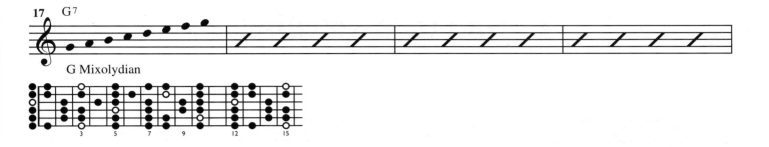

G Mixolydian

Dorian to Lydian

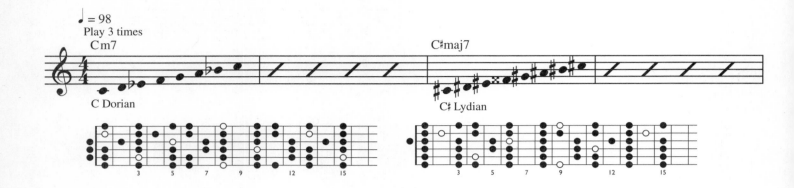

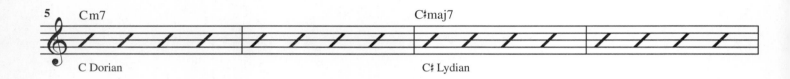

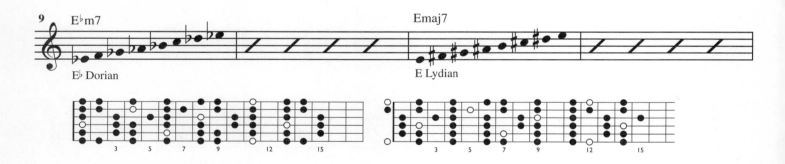

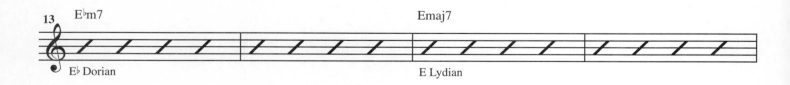

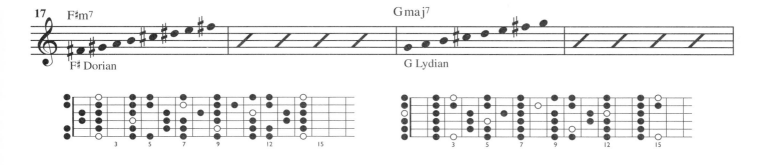

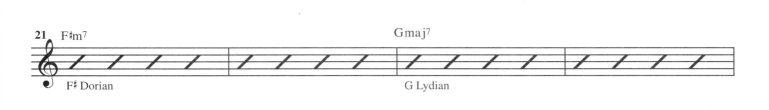

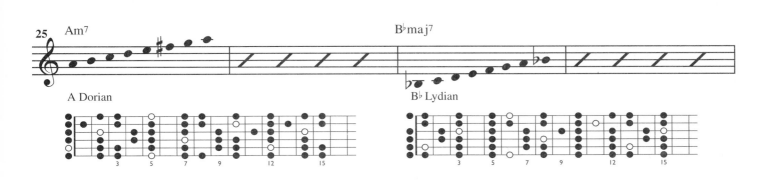

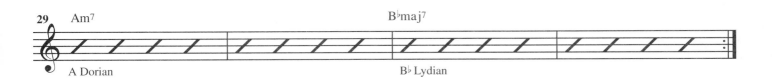

64

The World of D

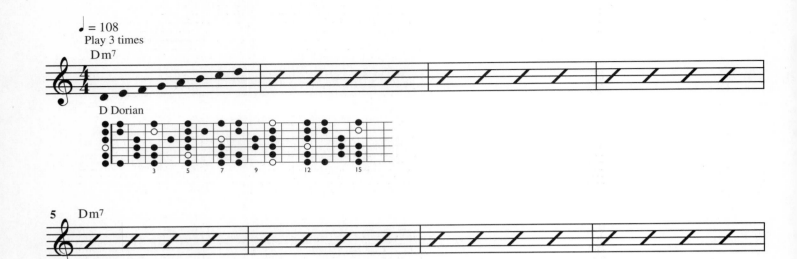

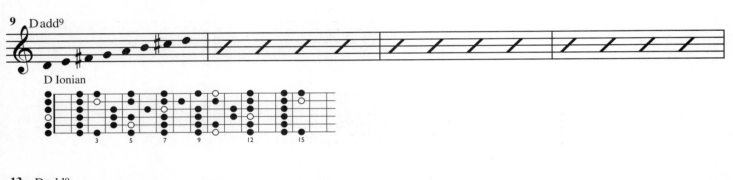

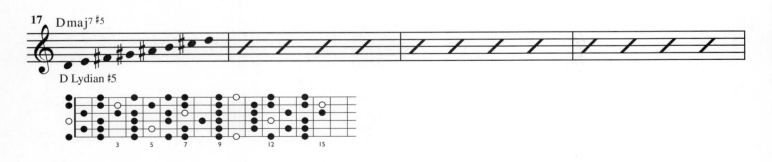

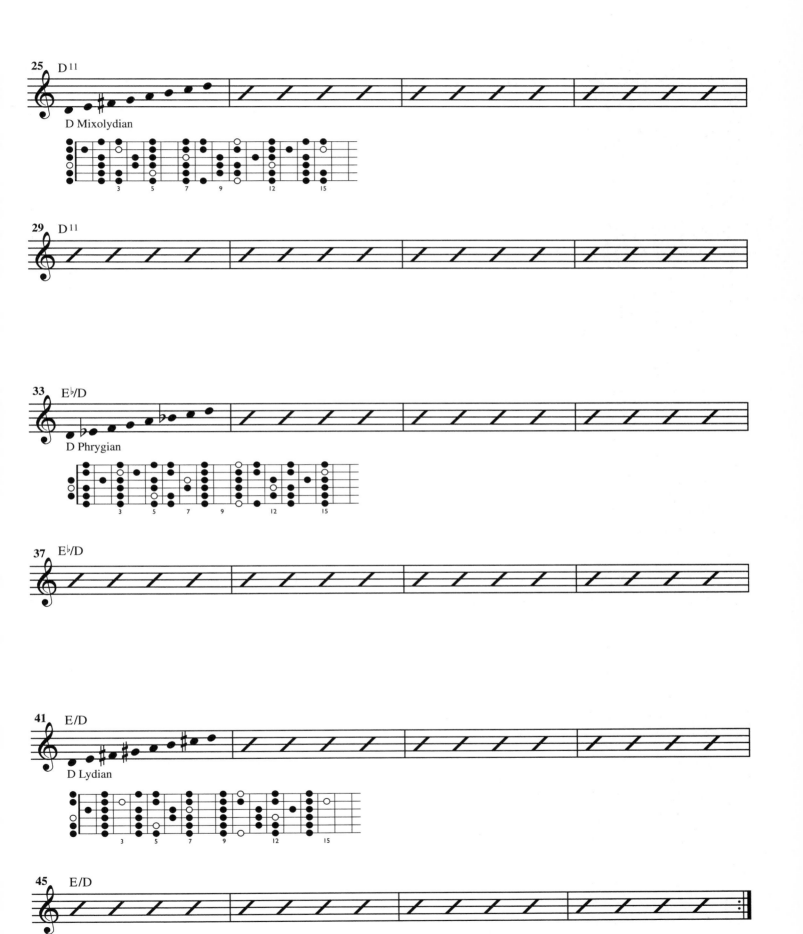

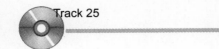

Triplet Feel

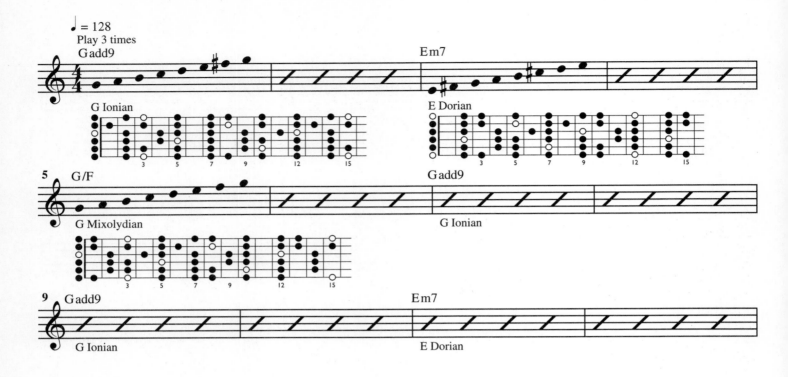

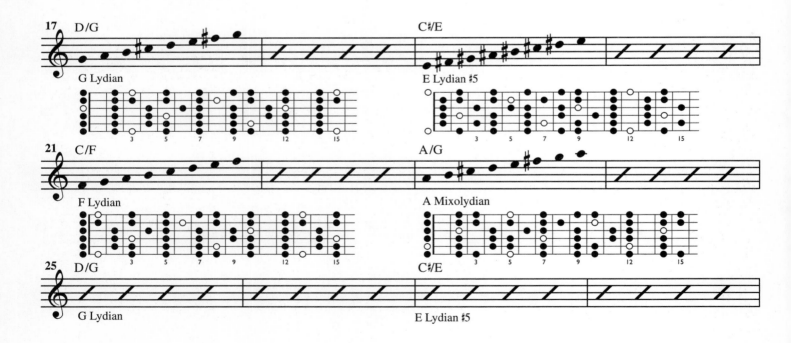

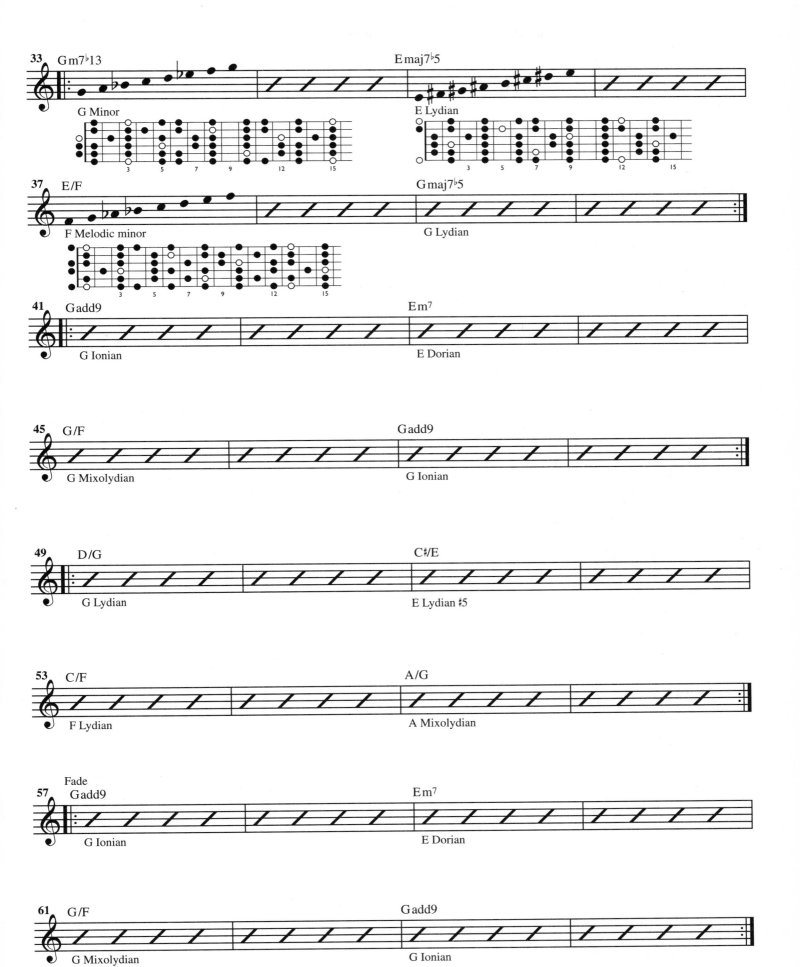

Diminished Blues

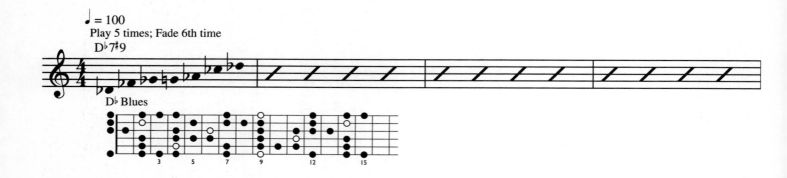

D♭ Blues

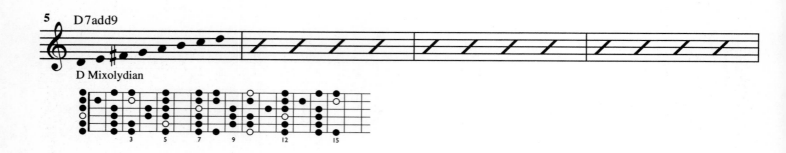

D Mixolydian

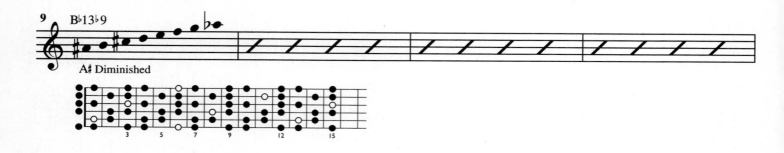

A♯ Diminished

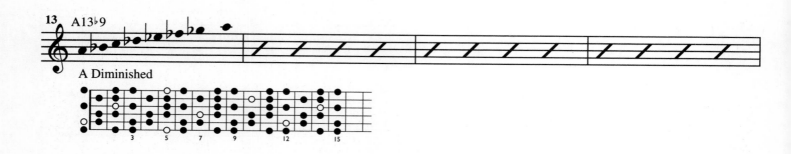

A Diminished

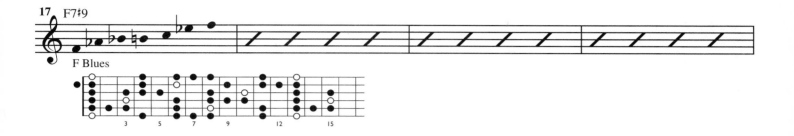

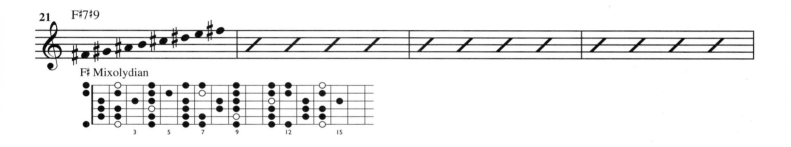

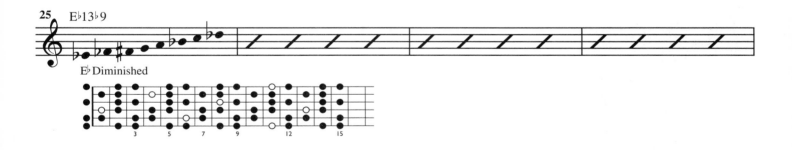

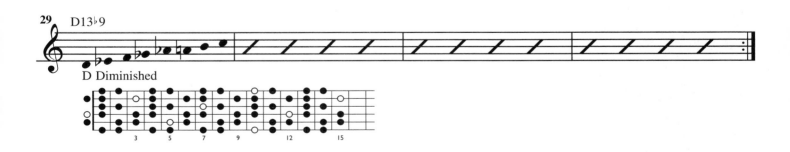

Dominant 7th City

♩ = 98
Play 5 times; Fade 6th time

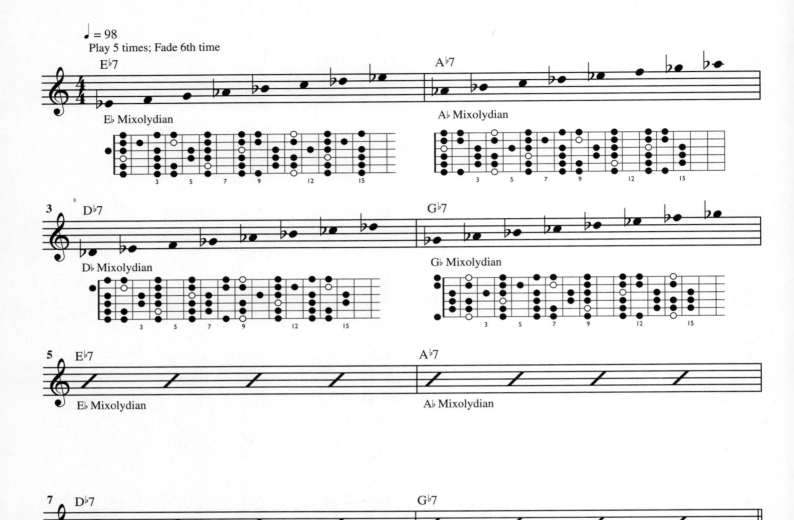

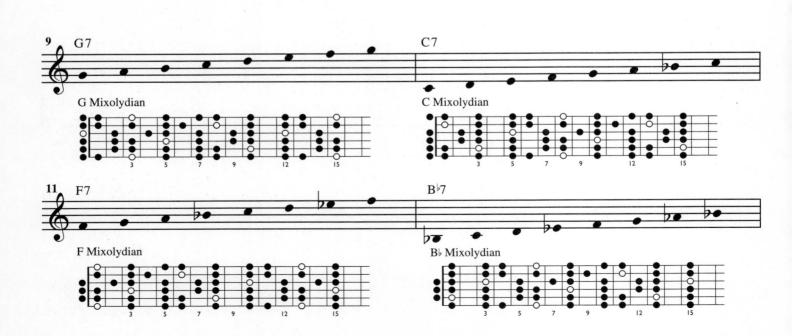

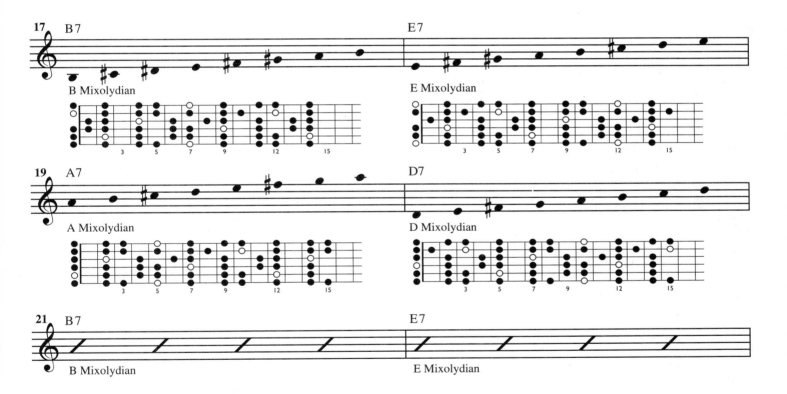

Whole Tone

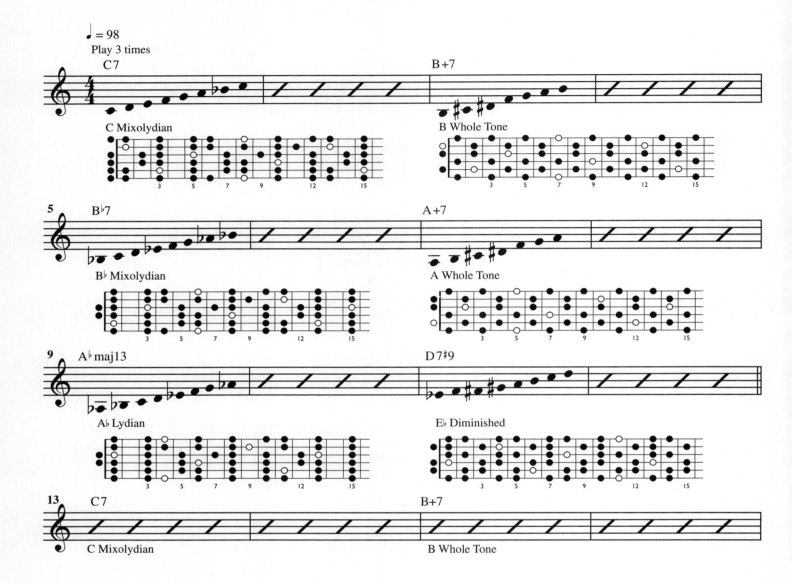

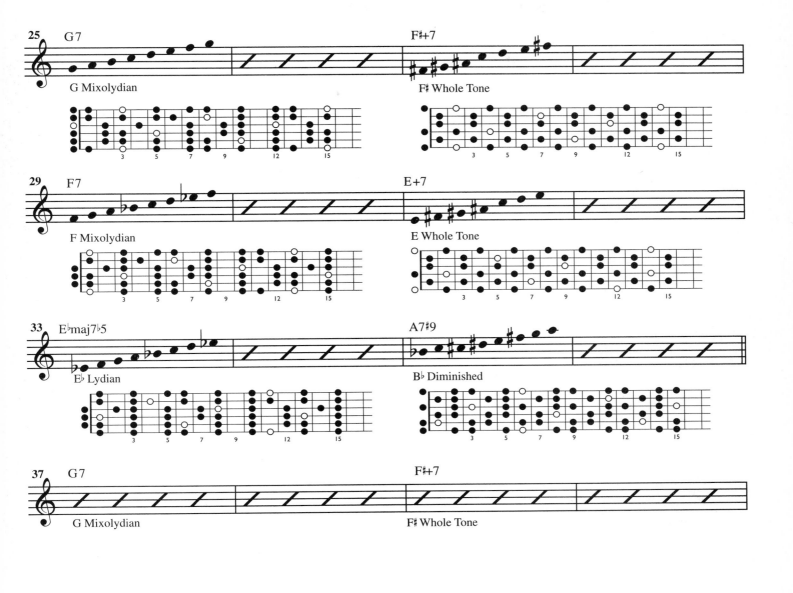

Mixolydian-Lydian-Diminished

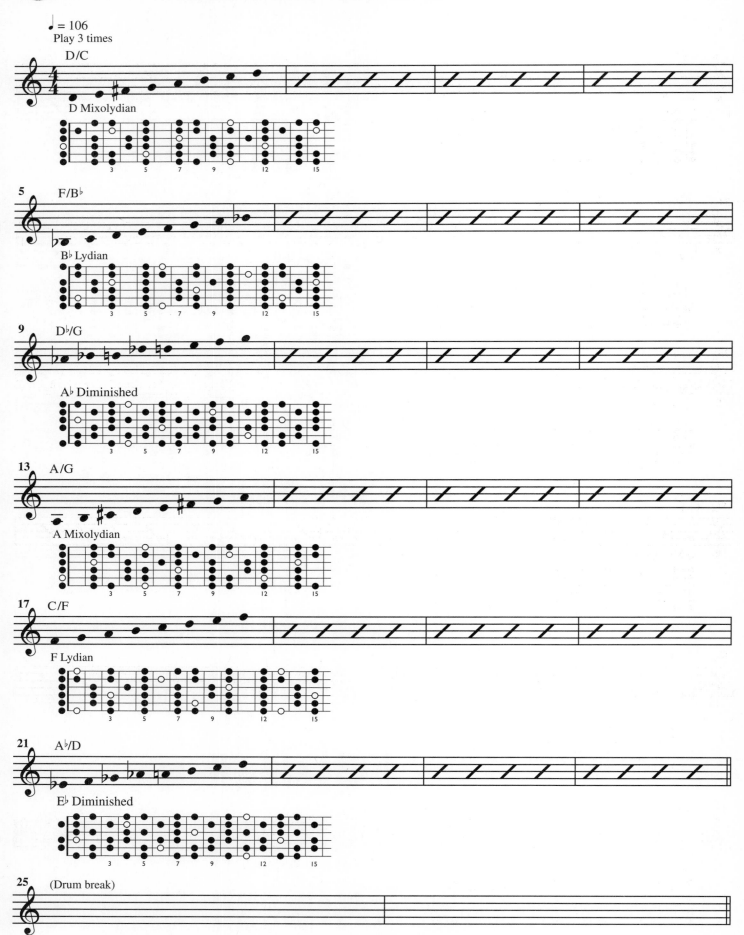

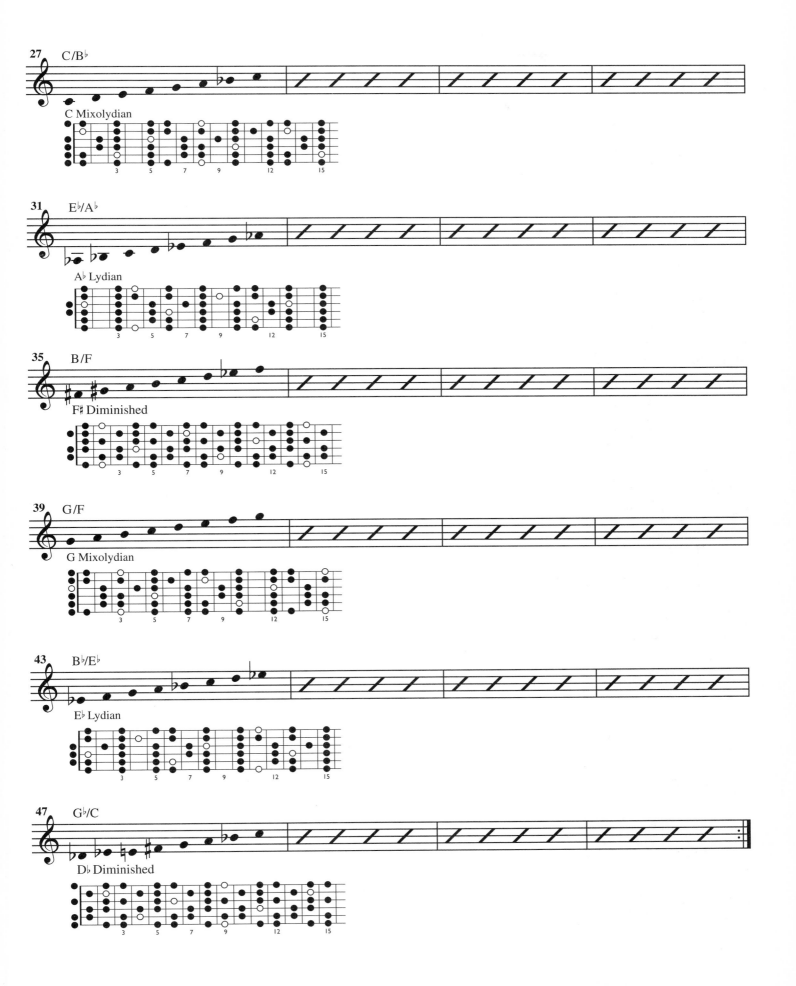

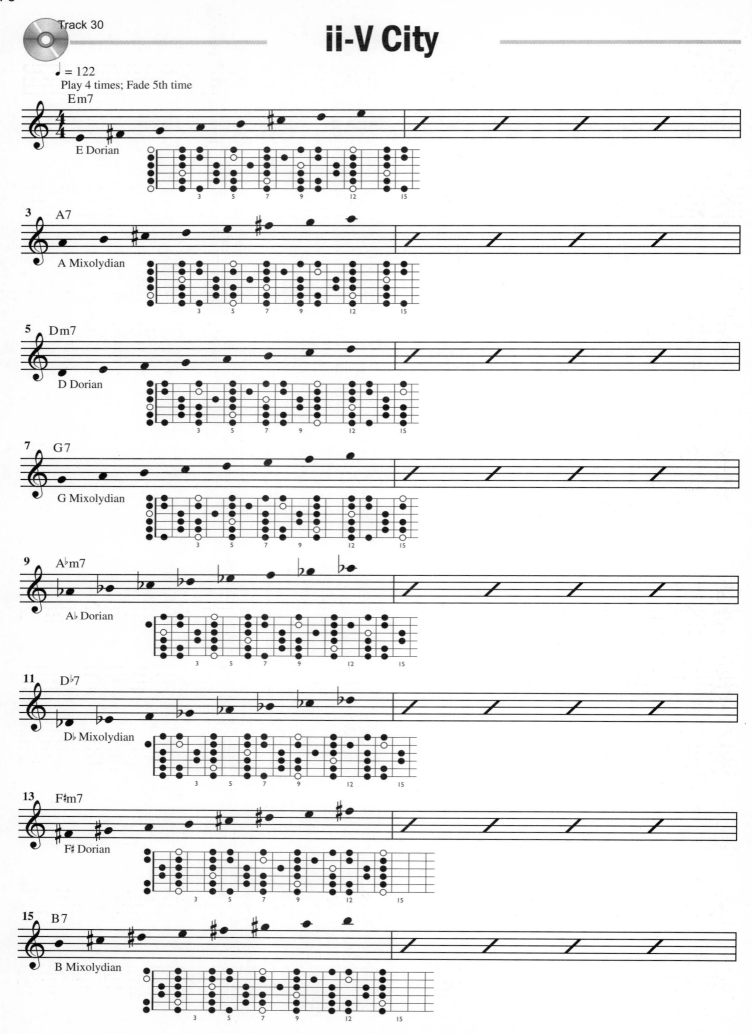

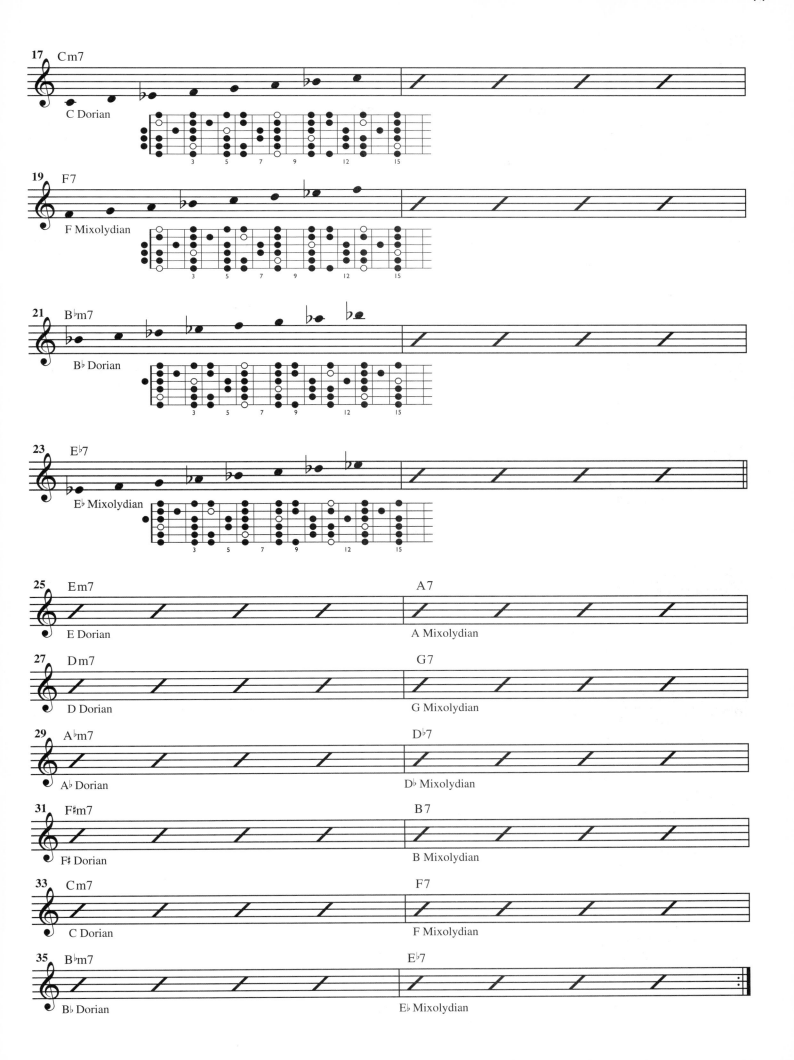

Diminished-Lydian ♭7

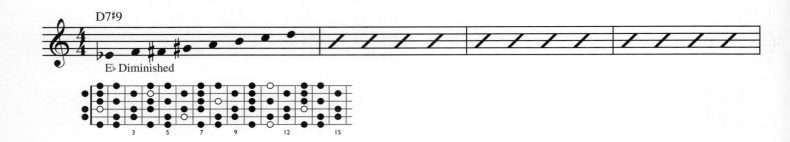

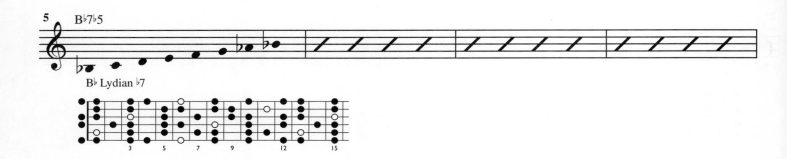

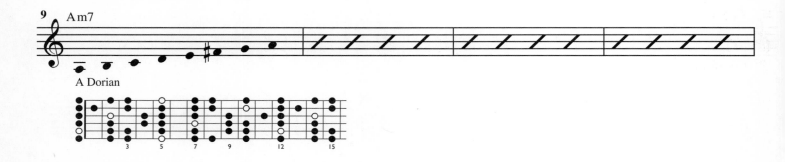

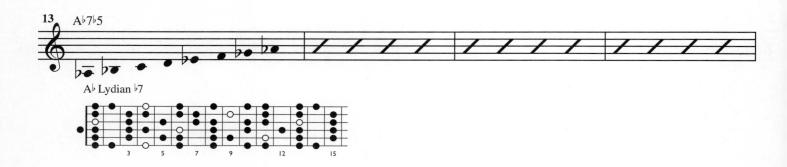

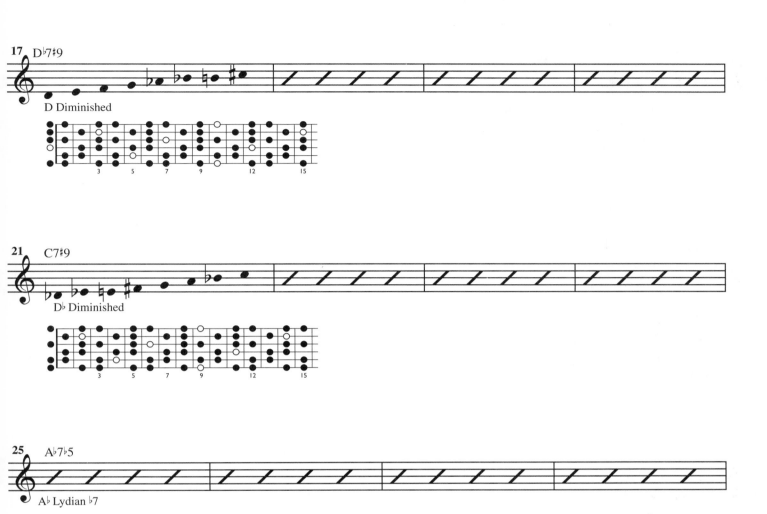

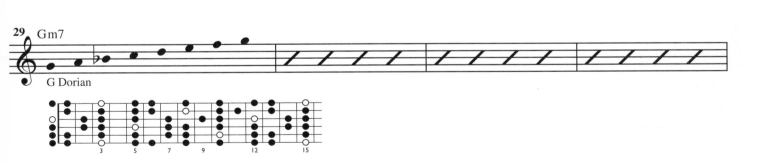

80

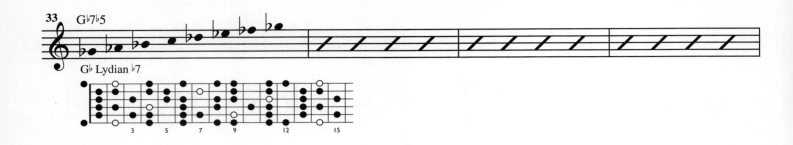

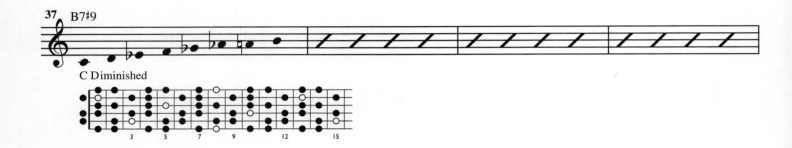

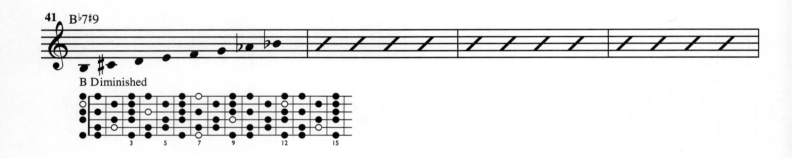

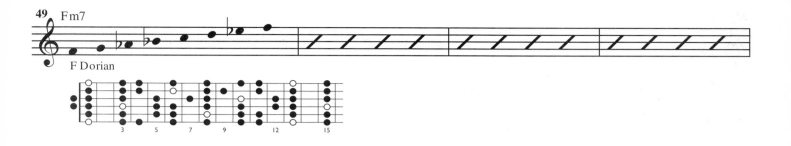

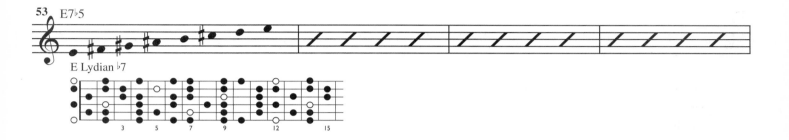

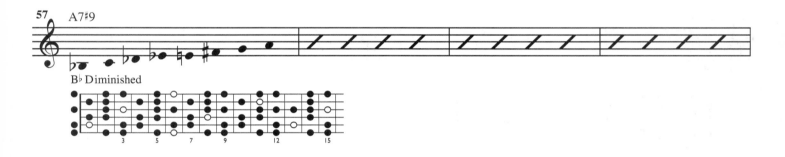

82

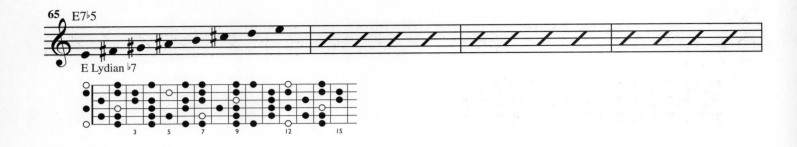

65 E7♭5

E Lydian ♭7

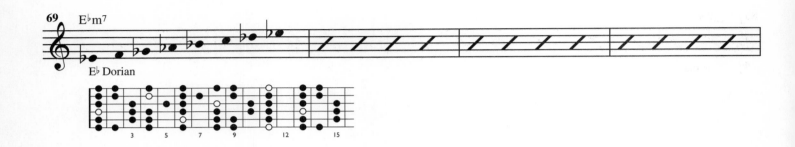

69 E♭m7

E♭ Dorian

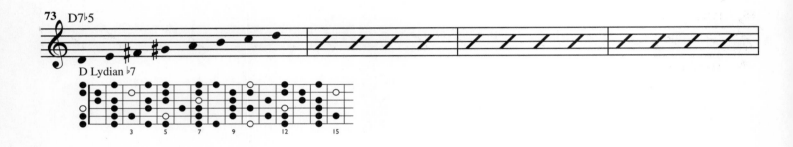

73 D7♭5

D Lydian ♭7

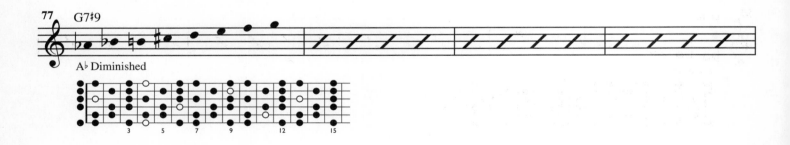

77 G7♯9

A♭ Diminished

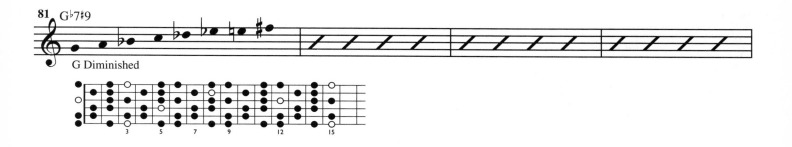

81 G♭7♯9

G Diminished

85 D7♭5

D Lydian ♭7

85 D7♭5

D Lydian ♭7

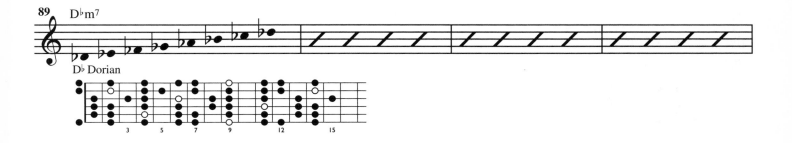

89 D♭m7

D♭ Dorian

93 C7♭5

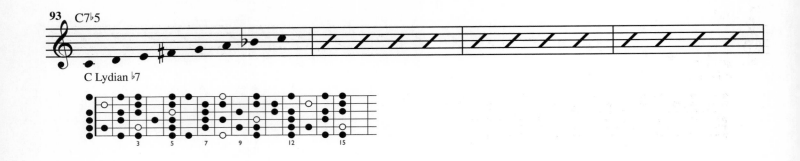

C Lydian ♭7

97 F7♯9

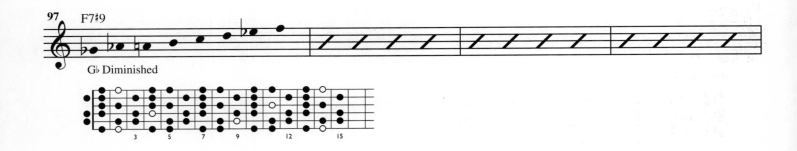

G♭ Diminished

101 E7♯9

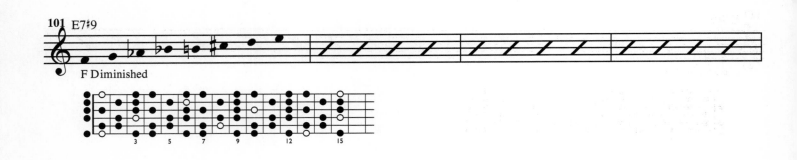

F Diminished

105 C7♭5

C Lydian ♭7

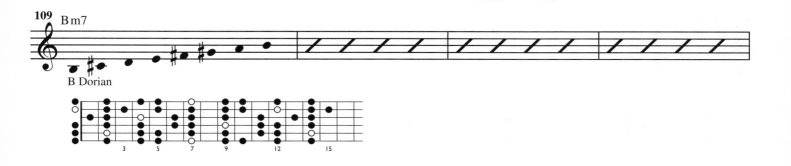

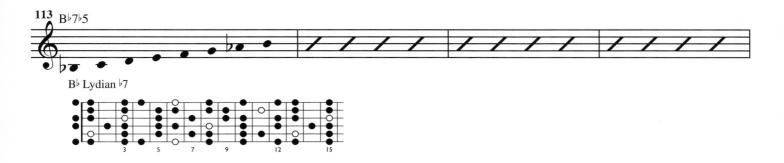

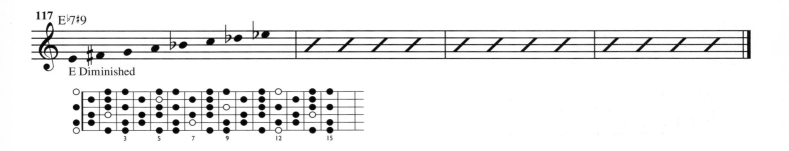

Notes

Guitar Fingerboard Chart
Frets 1–12

STRINGS

6th	5th	4th	3rd	2nd	1st
E	A	D	G	B	E

FRETS — **STRINGS**

Fret	6th	5th	4th	3rd	2nd	1st
Open	E	A	D	G	B	E
1st Fret	F	A#/Bb	D#/Eb	G#/Ab	C	F
2nd Fret	F#/Gb	B	E	A	C#/Db	F#/Gb
3rd Fret	G	C	F	A#/Bb	D	G
4th Fret	G#/Ab	C#/Db	F#/Gb	B	D#/Eb	G#/Ab
5th Fret	A	D	G	C	E	A
6th Fret	A#/Bb	D#/Eb	G#/Ab	C#/Db	F	A#/Bb
7th Fret	B	E	A	D	F#/Gb	B
8th Fret	C	F	A#/Bb	D#/Eb	G	C
9th Fret	C#/Db	F#/Gb	B	E	G#/Ab	C#/Db
10th Fret	D	G	C	F	A	D
11th Fret	D#/Eb	G#/Ab	C#/Db	F#/Gb	A#/Bb	D#/Eb
12th Fret	E	A	D	G	B	E

Fingerboard diagram (6th–1st strings: E A D G B E):

Fret	6th	5th	4th	3rd	2nd	1st
1st	F	A#/Bb	D#/Eb	G#/Ab	C	F
2nd	F#/Gb	B	E	A	C#/Db	F#/Gb
3rd	G	C	F	A#/Bb	D	G
4th	G#/Ab	C#/Db	F#/Gb	B	D#/Eb	G#/Ab
5th	A	D	G	C	E	A
6th	A#/Bb	D#/Eb	G#/Ab	C#/Db	F	A#/Bb
7th	B	E	A	D	F#/Gb	B
8th	C	F	A#/Bb	D#/Eb	G	C
9th	C#/Db	F#/Gb	B	E	G#/Ab	C#/Db
10th	D	G	C	F	A	D
11th	D#/Eb	G#/Ab	C#/Db	F#/Gb	A#/Bb	D#/Eb
12th	E	A	D	G	B	E